Bird Show

Written and illustrated by
Susan Stockdale

PEACHTREE
ATLANTA

For

Grant Charles Leonard

Published by
PEACHTREE PUBLISHING COMPANY INC.
1700 Chattahoochee Avenue
Atlanta, Georgia 30318-2112
PeachtreeBooks.com

First trade paperback edition published in 2022

Editor: Kathy Landwehr
Art director: Adela Pons

The illustrations were created in acrylic on paper.

On the cover: Grey-Crowned Crane

Printed and bound in September 2022 at Leo Paper, Heshan, China.
10 9 8 7 6 5 4 3 2 1 (hardcover)
10 9 8 7 6 5 4 3 2 1 (trade paperback)
HC ISBN: 978-1-68263-128-7
PB ISBN: 978-1-68263-646-6

Cataloging-in-Publication Data is available from the Library of Congress.

Big thanks to Dr. Carla Dove of the Smithsonian Institution's National Museum of Natural History for her close consultation with me on this book, always provided with such good cheer and enthusiasm. I am also grateful to Dr. Steven C. Latta of the National Aviary for his helpful research assistance.

I soar through the sky and like birds everywhere,

I'm decked out in feathers and wear them with flair.

I boast an outfit of every hue.

My coat has one color,

my jacket has two.

I flaunt a full skirt
of milky-white lace.

My apron is yellow,

my dress has a face.

I sport a vest that is dappled with dots.

My suit has white speckles,

my headdress has spots.

I flash a tailcoat
with curlicue flips.

My train has two paddles,

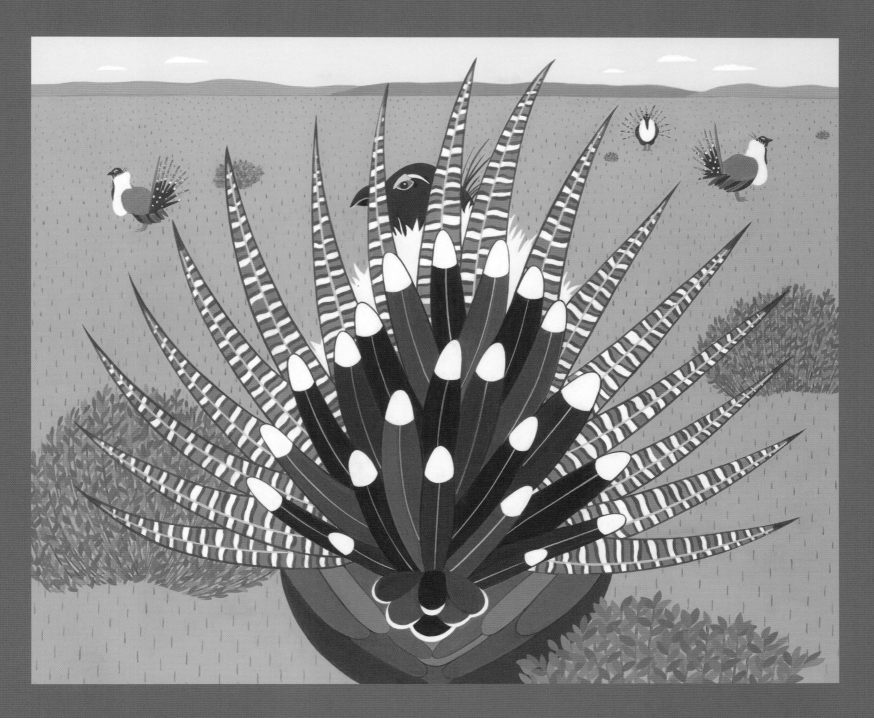

my fan has sharp tips.

I don an elegant, free-flowing gown.

My scarf stripes are curvy,

my plumes form a crown.

All of us dress
in our own special way,

and put on a fashion show every day!

Birds are the only living animals that have feathers. Most females have dull-colored feathers and fewer markings, so predators won't spot them while they care for their chicks. Most males feature brighter feathers to attract a female mate, as females prefer partners with more vibrant colors. Plain or showy, birds provide a dazzling display.

European Bee-eater

The vividly colored **European Bee-eater** uses its strong, sharp beak to pluck insects from the air.

Africa, Europe, and western Asia

Steller's Jay

One of North America's largest and loudest jays, the **Steller's Jay** flattens its distinctive crest when it is calm and raises it when it is agitated.

North and Central America

Mandarin Duck

To attract a mate, the male **Mandarin Duck** smooths and shakes his brilliant feathers.

*China, Japan, and southwestern Russia

Great Egret

During mating season, the male and female **Great Egret** extend long feather plumes from their back areas and spread them out like fans.

Africa, Asia, Australia, Europe, and North and South America

Northern Cardinal

The male **Northern Cardinal** whistles a lively song, stands upright, and sways back and forth to show off his crimson plumage to entice a female.

North and Central America

Yellow-breasted Chat

The **Yellow-breasted Chat** produces an unusual medley of hoots, whistles, cackles, and grunts. When mating, a male beats his wings fitfully before a female.

North and Central America

*The native range, which is the natural geographical home of the birds, is listed. The Mandarin Duck and the European Starling were introduced to the United States and elsewhere.

Superb Bird-of-Paradise

In a courtship display, the male **Superb Bird-of-Paradise** unfurls his feathers upward to form a black oval shape highlighted by bright feathers that resemble a blue smiling face.

New Guinea

Royal Flycatcher

When mating, the **Royal Flycatcher** lifts and flares its ornate crest and twists its head from side to side. It darts out from branches to catch and eat flying insects.

South America

Northern Flicker

Unlike most woodpeckers, the **Northern Flicker** primarily forages on the ground for food such as ants, beetle larvae, and berries.

North America

Wilson's Bird-of-Paradise

The male **Wilson's Bird-of-Paradise** weaves back and forth on a branch to lure a female.

Indonesia

European Starling

In winter, the **European Starling** joins a noisy flock of up to several thousand, which offers protection as predators find it hard to target individual birds.

*Europe, Asia, and northern Africa

Marvellous Spatuletail

During courtship, the male **Marvellous Spatuletail** hovers before a female and waves his tail feather discs, which are called "spatules."

Peru

Greater Sage-Grouse

The **Greater Sage-Grouse** is the largest grouse in North America. The male puffs out his chest, fans his tail, and struts to invite a mate.

North America

Grey-Crowned Crane

Both sexes of the **Grey-Crowned Crane** bow, jump, run, and toss sticks in a breeding display while inflating their red "gular sacs" to make booming calls.

Africa

Greater Bird-of-Paradise

To appeal to a female, the male **Greater Bird-of-Paradise** elevates and vibrates his large, bright plumes while flapping his wings rapidly.

Indonesia and Papua New Guinea

Resplendent Quetzal

During mating season, the male **Resplendent Quetzal** grows two vibrant "streamers" up to three feet long to attract a partner.

Central America and southern Mexico

Golden Pheasant

The male **Golden Pheasant** spreads his striking black-and-orange neck feathers over his face like a cape to woo a mate.

China

Scarlet Macaw

The **Scarlet Macaw**, one of the largest parrots in the world, mates for life. When flying, a couple stays close together with their wings almost touching.

Central and South America

Can you find the birds that belong to these colors and patterns?

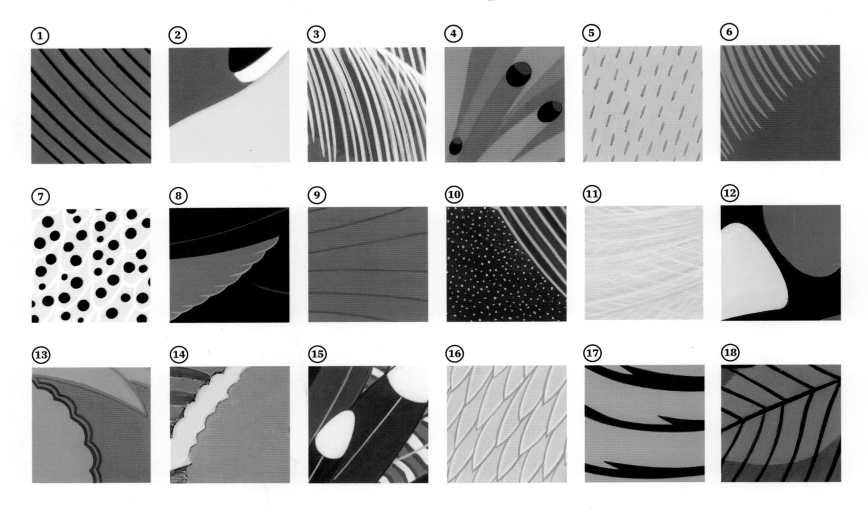

Turn the book upside down to read the correct answers.

1. Steller's Jay 2. Yellow-breasted Chat 3. Great Egret 4. Royal Flycatcher 5. European Bee-eater 6. Mandarin Duck 7. Northern Flicker 8. Superb Bird-of-Paradise 9. Northern Cardinal 10. European Starling 11. Greater Bird-of-Paradise 12. Wilson's Bird-of-Paradise 13. Resplendent Quetzal 14. Scarlet Macaw 15. Grey-Crowned Crane 16. Greater Sage-Grouse 17. Golden Pheasant 18. Marvellous Spatuletail